HOLY FAMILY
PRAYER BOOK

Bart Tesoriero, Teresa West

ISBN: 978-1-61796-364-3
Artwork ©2021 Michael Adams
Text ©2021 Aquinas Press
Printed in China

TABLE OF CONTENTS

The Sign of the Cross

In the name of the Father and of the Son, and of the Holy Spirit, Amen.

The Lord's Prayer

Our Father, Who art in heaven, hallowed be Thy Name; Thy Kingdom come; Thy Will be done on earth as it is in heaven.

Give us this day our daily bread; and forgive us our trespasses, as we forgive those who trespass against us; and lead us not into temptation, but deliver us from evil. Amen.

The Hail Mary

Hail Mary, full of grace, the Lord is with thee; Blessed art thou among women, and blessed is the fruit of thy womb, Jesus.

Holy Mary, Mother of God, pray for us sinners, now and at the hour of our death. Amen.

Glory Be

Glory be to the Father, and to the Son, and to the Holy Spirit; as it was in the beginning, is now, and ever shall be, world without end. Amen.

Grace Before Meals

Bless us, O Lord, and these Thy gifts, which we are about to receive from Thy bounty, through Christ our Lord. Amen.

Grace After Meals

We give You thanks, O Lord, for these and all Thy gifts, which we have received from Thy bounty, through Christ our Lord. Amen.

Daily Consecration to Mary

O Mary, my Queen and my Mother, I give myself entirely to you. And as proof of my filial devotion, I consecrate to you this day my eyes, my ears, my mouth, my heart, my whole being without reserve. Wherefore, good Mother, as I am your own, keep me and guard me as your property and possession. Amen.

Morning Offering

O Jesus, through the Immaculate Heart of Mary, I offer You my prayers, works, joys and sufferings of this day, in union with the Holy Sacrifice of the Mass offered throughout the world, in reparation for all my sins, and for the sins of the whole world.

I offer this day for all the intentions of Your Sacred Heart, for the intentions of the Immaculate Heart of our Mother Mary, for the intentions of my family, friends, relatives, and benefactors, and for the intentions of our Holy Father. Amen.

The Angelus

V. The Angel of the Lord declared unto Mary.
R. And she conceived by the Holy Spirit.
(Hail Mary...)

V. Behold the handmaid of the Lord.
R. Be it done unto me according to thy word.
(Hail Mary...)

V. And the Word was made Flesh.
R. And dwelt among us.
(Hail Mary...)

V. Pray for us, O Holy Mother of God.
R. That we may be made worthy of the promises of Christ.

Let us pray: Pour forth, we beseech Thee, O Lord, Thy grace into our hearts; that we to whom the Incarnation of Christ, Thy Son, was made known by the message of an Angel, may by His Passion and Cross be brought to the glory of His Resurrection. Through the same Christ our Lord. Amen.

Evening Prayer

Watch, O Lord, with those who wake, or watch, or weep tonight, and give Your Angels and Saints charge over those who sleep. Tend Your sick ones, O Lord Christ. Rest Your weary ones, Bless Your dying ones; Soothe Your suffering ones, Pity Your afflicted ones; Shield Your joyous ones, And all for Your love's sake. Amen. –Saint Augustine

O God, come to my assistance; O Lord make haste to help me. Glory be to the Father, and to the Son, and the Holy Spirit; as it was in the beginning, is now and ever shall be, world without end. Amen.

Make a short review of the day, briefly recalling with gratitude the good things that have happened, and repenting in sincere sorrow for the sins you have committed.

O my God, I thank You for having preserved me today and for having given me so many blessings and graces. I renew my dedication to You and ask Your pardon for all my sins. In Jesus' name. Amen.

Prayer to Saint Michael the Archangel

Saint Michael the Archangel, defend us in battle. Be our protection against the wickedness and snares of the devil. May God rebuke him, we humbly pray; and do thou, O Prince of the heavenly host, by the power of God, cast into hell Satan and all the evil spirits, who wander through the world seeking the ruin of souls. Amen.

Prayer to Your Guardian Angel

O Angel of God, my Guardian dear, to whom God's love commits me here, ever this day (or night) be at my side, to light and guard, to rule and guide, Amen.

Memorare

Remember, O most gracious Virgin Mary, that never was it known, that anyone who fled to thy protection, implored thy help or sought thy intercession, was left unaided. Inspired by this confidence, I fly unto thee, O Virgin of virgins, my Mother. To thee do I come, before thee I stand, sinful and sorrowful; O Mother of the Word Incarnate, despise not my petitions, but in thy mercy hear and answer me. Amen.

Hail, Holy Queen

Hail, holy Queen, Mother of mercy; our life, our sweetness and our hope. To thee do we cry, poor banished children of Eve. To thee do we send up our sighs, mourning and weeping in this valley of tears. Turn then, most gracious Advocate, thine eyes of mercy toward us, and after this our exile show unto us the blessed fruit of thy womb, Jesus. O clement, O loving, O sweet Virgin Mary.
V. Pray for us, O Holy Mother of God;
R. That we made be made worthy of the promises of Christ.

Memorare to Saint Joseph

Remember, O most chaste spouse of the
Virgin Mary, that never was it known that
anyone who implored your help and sought
your intercession were left unassisted.
Full of confidence in your power I fly unto
you and beg your protection.
Despise not O Guardian of the Redeemer
my humble supplication, but in your bounty,
hear and answer me. Amen.

Act of Consecration to Saint Joseph

O dearest Saint Joseph, I consecrate myself to
your honor and give myself to you, that you
may always be my father, my protector and my
guide in the way of salvation.
Obtain for me a greater purity of heart and
fervent love of the interior life.
After your example may I do all my actions
for the greater glory of God, in union with
the Divine Heart of Jesus and the Immaculate
Heart of Mary. O Blessed Saint Joseph, pray
for me, that I may share in the peace and joy
of your holy death. Amen.

Prayer for Husband and Wife

Thank You dear Lord for the gift of marriage, through which we are made one flesh. Through the intercession of Joseph and Mary, strengthen and renew us daily in our sacrament of marriage. Bless us, according to Your Will, with the gift of children, and help us to be good parents. Keep us faithful in marriage and let us be living examples of Christian life.

Give us help in our difficulties, which can at times be very great, for indeed the gate is narrow and the way is hard that leads to eternal life. Pour Your love out afresh in our hearts through the Holy Spirit who has been given to us. Help us draw grace and love from the fountain of the Eucharist and overcome with humble perseverance our weaknesses and sins in the Sacrament of Reconciliation. In our unity and fruitfulness, may we be witnesses to Your love and a sign of Your truth. We ask this through Christ Our Lord, Amen.

A Prayer to Saint Joseph
For One's Children

O glorious Saint Joseph, to you God committed the care of His only begotten Son. We ask you to take under your special protection the children God has given us. Through Baptism they became children of God and members of His Church.

We consecrate them to you today, that through this consecration they may become your foster children. Guard them, guide their steps in life, and form their hearts after the hearts of Jesus and Mary.

Saint Joseph, who felt the frantic worry of a parent when Jesus was lost, protect our dear children for time and eternity. Be their father and counselor. Let them, like Jesus, grow in age as well as in wisdom and grace. Preserve them from the corruption of this world, and pray that one day we will be united with them in Heaven forever. Amen.

Prayer for Family Healing

Dear God, thank You for the gift of our family. You have called us to love one another, yet we are tempted to fight, bicker, and be selfish. Give us Your presence today and the gift of Your Holy Spirit. Make us instruments of Your peace.

Help us to love and serve one another in humility. Help us to listen to one another, to share, and to confront when necessary. Remind us that growth is a process that takes time and patience. Help us encourage one another to be all You created us to be. We trust in You and surrender ourselves and our family to You, confident that You will work out all things to the good for those who are called according to Your purpose. We ask this in Jesus' name. Amen.

Prayer for One's Family

O dear Jesus, I humbly implore You to grant Your special graces to our family. May our home be the shrine of peace, purity, love, labor and faith. I beg You, dear Jesus, to protect and bless all of us, absent and present, living and dead.

O Mary, loving Mother of Jesus, and our Mother, pray to Jesus for our family, for all the families of the world, to guard the cradle of the newborn, the schools of the young and their vocations.

Blessed Saint Joseph, holy guardian of Jesus and Mary, assist us by your prayers in all the necessities of life. Ask of Jesus that special grace which He granted to you, to watch over our home at the pillow of the sick and the dying, so that with Mary and with you, heaven may find our family unbroken in the Sacred Heart of Jesus. Amen.

Prayer of Pope Pius XII for Families

O Lord, God of goodness and mercy, Who in the midst of an evil and sinful world presented to the society of the redeemed the Holy Family of Nazareth as a spotless mirror of piety, justice and love, behold how the family is being undermined on all sides, every effort being made to desecrate it by stripping it of faith, religion, and morals.

Regard the work of Your own hands. Safeguard in our homes the domestic virtues, for these alone will ensure us harmony and peace.

Come and stir up the champions of the family. Grant through the efforts of these apostles, that the home favored by You with many blessings may again become an object of esteem and love in the minds and hearts of all. Amen.

Family Prayer
For World Meeting of Families

God, our Father, we are brothers and sisters
in Jesus Your Son, one family in the Spirit of
your love. Bless us with the joy of love. Make
us patient and kind, gentle and generous,
welcoming to those in need. Help us to
live Your forgiveness and peace. Protect all
families with Your loving care, especially
those for whom we now pray:
*(Pause and remember family members and others
by name.)*

Increase our faith, strengthen our hope, keep
us safe in Your love, make us always grateful
for the gift of life that we share. This we ask,
through Christ our Lord. Amen.

Mary, mother and guide, pray for us.
Saint Joseph, father and protector, pray for us.
Saints Joachim and Anne, pray for us.
Saints Louis and Zélie Martin, pray for us.

Consecration of Our Family to Mary

O Mary, our Mother, we come to you as a family and consecrate ourselves to your most Immaculate Heart. We place our trust in your powerful intercession. Teach us as a mother teaches her children. We are ready to respond to you and follow your way, for it leads to your Son, Jesus. Embrace us with your maternal protection. Be with us when trials beset us and we are confused and worried.

Help us realize that we are never without your concern and maternal love; help us to rely on that love even if we feel unlovable. Help us to avoid being critical of one another's shortcomings; and if at times we are, place a motherly finger gently on our lips and bid us to stop. Help us appreciate each other as you certainly appreciated the quiet strength of your spouse Joseph and the divine wonder of your holy Child. Amen.

Litany of Saint Joseph, Patron of Families

V. Lord, have mercy. **R. Christ, have mercy.**
V. Lord, have mercy. **R. Christ, have mercy.**
V. Christ, hear us. **R. Christ, graciously hear us.**
V. God the Father of Heaven,
R. Have mercy on us.
V. God the Son, Redeemer of the world,
R. Have mercy on us.
V. God the Holy Spirit, R. Have mercy on us.
V. Holy Trinity, One God,
R. Have mercy on us.

R. Pray for us.

Holy Mary,
Saint Joseph,
Renowned offspring of David,
Light of patriarchs,
Spouse of the Mother of God,
Chaste guardian of the Virgin,
Foster-father of the Son of God,
Diligent protector of Christ,
Head of the holy family,

Joseph most just, **R. Pray for us.**
Joseph most chaste,
Joseph most prudent,
Joseph most brave,
Joseph most obedient,
Joseph most faithful,
Mirror of patience,
Lover of poverty,
Model of artisans,
Glory of home life,
Guardian of virgins,
Pillar of families,
Solace of the wretched,
Hope of the sick,
Patron of the dying,
Terror of demons,
Protector of the holy Church,
V. Lamb of God, who takes away the sins of the world,
R. Spare us, O Lord.
V. Lamb of God, who takes away the sins of the world,
R. Graciously hear us, O Lord.
V. Lamb of God, who takes away the sins of the world,
R. Have mercy on us.

V. He made him lord of His House.
R. And ruler of all His possessions.

Let us pray. O God, who in Your infinite providence chose blessed Joseph to be the spouse of Your own most holy Mother, grant, we beseech You, that we may deserve to have him as our intercessor in heaven, whom we venerate on earth as our protector; You who live and reign world without end. Amen.

Novena Prayer to Saint Joseph

O Saint Joseph whose protection is so great, so strong, so prompt before the Throne of God, I place in you all my interests and desires. O Saint Joseph, please help me by your powerful intercession and obtain for me from your Divine Son all spiritual blessings through Jesus Christ, Our Lord; so that having engaged here below your Heavenly power I may offer my thanksgiving and praise to the most loving of Fathers. O Saint Joseph, I never weary contemplating you and Jesus asleep in your arms. I dare not approach while He reposes near your heart. Press Him in my name and kiss His fine Head for me, and ask Him to return the Kiss when I draw my dying breath. Saint Joseph, Patron of departing souls, pray for us. Amen.

Litany to Mary, Queen of the Family

There are so many families in desperate need. They require your protection. They need your guidance.
Mary, Queen of Families, we implore you!

There are so many families who have become lax in their faith and even entangled in error. They need your clarity and security. They need your courage and strong faith.
Mary, Queen of Families, we implore you!

There are so many families who lack spiritual and material possessions. They need your help. They need your intercession.
Mary, Queen of Families, we implore you!

There are so many families who have become too weak in order to resist temptations. They need your strength. They need your purity.
Mary, Queen of Families, we implore you!

There are so many families who experience

difficulties in educating their children. They need your motherly love. They need your educative hand.

Mary, Queen of Families, we implore you!

There are so many families torn apart through a loss of true love. They need your goodness. They need your loving understanding.

Mary, Queen of Families, we implore you!

Ancient Prayer to the Virgin Mary

We turn to you for protection, holy Mother of God. Listen to our prayers, and help us in our needs. Save us from every danger, O glorious and blessed Virgin. Amen.

Prayers to the Holy Spirit

Come, Holy Spirit, fill the hearts of Your faithful and enkindle in them the fire of Your love.

V. Send forth Your Spirit and they shall be created.

R. And You shall renew the face of the earth.

O God, Who by the light of the Holy Spirit, has instructed the hearts of the faithful, grant us in the same Spirit to be truly wise and ever to rejoice in His consolation. Through Christ our Lord. Amen.

Prayer of Saint Anthony of Padua

O God, send forth Your Holy Spirit into my heart that I may perceive; into my mind that I may remember; and into my soul that I may meditate. Inspire me to speak with piety, holiness, tenderness, and mercy.

Teach, guide, and direct my thoughts and senses from beginning to end. May Your grace ever help and correct me, and may I be strengthened now with wisdom from on high, for the sake of Your infinite mercy. Amen.

Prayer for the Gifts of the Spirit

Lord and Giver of Life, Father of the Poor, You who pour forth Your Sevenfold gifts through the Sacrament of Confirmation, hear us as we pray: Spirit of sonship, grant to us *Fear of the Lord* that we might stand in Your presence with wonder and awe, and *Piety* to draw our hearts to recognize that You are our Father and we are Your children. Keep us in step with You by sending us *Counsel* to know Your Will for our lives, *Wisdom* to apply that Will, and *Fortitude* to do Your Will.

Dear Holy Spirit, beloved of our soul and inner flame that keeps us warm and loving, grant us *Knowledge* to know Your truth in our heart, and *Understanding* to comprehend what You have revealed. Heavenly Father, may these gifts conform us to the image of your Son, Jesus, the firstborn among many. In Jesus' name we pray. Amen.

Venerable Prayer to the Holy Family

Most loving Jesus, who blessed with peace and happiness the family which Your Father chose for You, look upon this household.

We implore Your mercy. Remember that we belong to You; we have dedicated and devoted ourselves to You. Look upon us in Your loving kindness, preserve us from danger, give us help in time of need, and grant us the grace to persevere in following the example of Your Holy Family.

O Mary, sweet Mother, we have recourse to your intercession, knowing that your divine Son will hear your prayers for us.

O glorious patriarch Saint Joseph, assist us by your powerful mediation, and offer through the hands of Mary, your spouse, our prayers to Jesus. Amen.

Prayer for Our Family
To Saints Joachim and Anne,
Parents of Mary, Grandparents of Jesus

Like Zachariah and Elizabeth, Anne and Joachim were advanced in years and childless. God answered their impassioned prayers with...Mary!

Good parents of Mary, you who trusted in God's will, help us to respect and rejoice in God's gift of fertility. Teach us to rejoice in our children and nurture them with love and instruction in the faith. When life seems barren, help us to trust in fruits of faith. When our days seem lifeless, show us the eternal youthfulness of life in Christ.

When we are selfish, remind us both to serve one another within our family and to serve others as a family. When we are afraid or timid, help us to trust. When we are ashamed, remind us that we are God's children and that a sincere, repentant heart will bring God's loving forgiveness. Amen.

Family Psalms

Psalm 23

The Lord is my shepherd; I shall not want.

He makes me lie down in green pastures;

He leads me beside the still waters.

He restores my soul. He leads me in the paths of

righteousness for His name's sake. Yea, though I

walk through the valley of the shadow of death,

I will fear no evil: for You are with me;

Your rod and Your staff, they comfort me.

You prepare a table before me in the presence of my

enemies. You anoint my forehead with oil;

my cup overflows.

Surely goodness and mercy shall follow me

all the days of my life; and I will dwell

in the house of the Lord forever.

Psalm 127

Unless the LORD build the house, they labor in vain who build. Unless the LORD guard the city, in vain does the guard keep watch. It is vain for you to rise early and put off your rest at night, To eat bread earned by hard toil–all this God gives to his beloved in sleep. Children too are a gift from the LORD, the fruit of the womb, a reward. Like arrows in the hand of a warrior are the children born in one's youth. Blessed are they whose quivers are full. They will never be shamed contending with foes at the gate.

Psalm 128

Blessed are all who fear the LORD, and who walk in his ways. What your hands provide you will enjoy; you will be blessed and prosper: Your wife will be like a fruitful vine within your home, Your children like young olive plants around your table. Just so will the man be blessed who fears the LORD. May the LORD bless you from Zion; may you see Jerusalem's prosperity all the days of your life, and live to see your children's children. Peace upon Israel!

Prayer for Our Extended Family

Loving God, we pray for our extended family: grandparents, great-grandparents, aunts, uncles, cousins, mothers- fathers- sisters and brothers-in-law, and all those with whom we feel a closeness that makes them virtually one of the family.

Life gets busy—too busy, we often feel—and it's difficult to find time to stay in contact with them as closely as we would like. Yet when we take time to think of it, we realize that we owe them a great deal for the influence they have been on our lives.

Prompt us to let them know we value them, even if it's simply with an unexpected phone call or note. Be with them in their difficulties, especially those who are growing older. Reward them for all the good they've done. And may we join with them at the heavenly banquet You have prepared for all Your children. In Jesus' name. Amen.

The Family Rosary

The Rosary is the most popular private devotion and method of meditation in the Catholic Church, joining us to God through Mary, our mother and intercessor. In the Rosary we ask Mary, the Mother of Jesus, to pray for us now, and at the hour of our death. In a special way, to pray the Family Rosary is to invite Mary into our home, into our family, into the most intimate heart of our family, to be with us.

How to Pray the Family Rosary

- Give each member of the family his or her own rosary. If possible, have the rosaries blessed by a priest or deacon.
- Set a regular time—usually in the evening, after dinner, works best for many families.
- Set a regular space, preferably around the family altar, with a lit candle.
- Start by praying one decade each evening, and increase to a whole Rosary over time.
- Involve everyone. Let the children lead the prayers or offer intentions, as they are able.

How to Pray the Rosary

- Begin by making the Sign of the Cross and praying the "Apostles' Creed," while you hold the crucifix.
- Pray one "Our Father" on the first bead, three "Hail Marys" on the next three beads for the virtues of Faith, Hope, and Charity, and finish with a "Glory Be to the Father."
- Announce the first Mystery and meditate on it while praying an "Our Father" on the large bead, ten "Hail Marys" on the smaller beads, and finishing with a "Glory Be to the Father." This is one decade.
- If you wish, add the "Fatima Prayer" after the "Glory Be."
- Continue in this way until all you have prayed all five decades. To finish, pray the "Hail Holy Queen."

Fatima Prayer

O my Jesus, forgive us our sins; save us from the fires of hell. Lead all souls to Heaven, especially those most in need of Your mercy.

The Apostles' Creed

I believe in God, the Father almighty, Creator of heaven and earth, and in Jesus Christ, His only Son, our Lord, Who was conceived by the Holy Spirit, born of the Virgin Mary, suffered under Pontius Pilate, was crucified, died, and was buried.

He descended into hell. The third day He arose again from the dead. He ascended into heaven and sits at the right hand of God the Father Almighty, from whence He shall come to judge the living and the dead.

I believe in the Holy Spirit, the Holy Catholic Church, the communion of saints, the forgiveness of sins, the resurrection of the body, and life everlasting. Amen.

Prayer After the Rosary

O God, whose only-begotten Son, by His life, death and resurrection, has purchased for us the rewards of eternal life; grant, we beseech Thee, that meditating upon these mysteries of the Most Holy Rosary of the Blessed Virgin Mary, we may imitate what they contain and obtain what they promise, through the same Christ our Lord. Amen.

The Joyful Mysteries
(Monday and Saturday)

THE ANNUNCIATION
Dear Mother Mary, through your intercession, help me say yes to God in all He asks of me, with a willing heart.

THE VISITATION
Dear Mother Mary, through your intercession, help me to reach out and care for others with love.

THE BIRTH OF OUR LORD
Dear Mother Mary, reveal the love of Your Son Jesus in my heart, that I may be ever close to Him.

THE PRESENTATION OF JESUS
Dear Mother Mary, help me pray in faith, obey in trust, and wait in hope, that Our Lord will fulfill all His promises and bring me His salvation.

THE FINDING OF JESUS

Dear Mother Mary, help me witness in all my life to the deep and strong love God has for me, and to seek Him with all my heart.

The Luminous Mysteries
(Thursday)

THE BAPTISM OF JESUS
IN THE JORDAN

Dear Mother Mary, in the Father's embrace Jesus was able to accept and follow His vocation. Help me also receive the Father's love, and do my best to fulfill my mission as well.

THE WEDDING AT CANA

Dear Mary, at your request Jesus changed water into wine and opened the hearts of His disciples to faith. Help me also trust in God to turn the water of my life into the wine of His presence.

THE PROCLAMATION
OF THE KINGDOM

Dear Mother Mary, help me to hear and respond wholeheartedly to the Word of God so powerfully proclaimed by Jesus.

THE TRANSFIGURATION OF JESUS

Dear Mother Mary, help me revere Christ always in my heart.

THE INSTITUTION OF THE EUCHARIST

Dear Mother Mary, may I always be grateful for this precious gift.

The Sorrowful Mysteries
(Tuesday, Friday)

THE AGONY IN THE GARDEN

Dear Mother Mary, please pray with me for the grace to accept the sufferings and struggles of my life, trusting that God is able to work it all out for the good.

THE SCOURGING AT THE PILLAR

Dear Mother Mary, may I seek to love rather than be loved, and to shine the warmth of Jesus on all I meet.

THE CROWNING WITH THORNS

Dear Mother Mary, help me remember Jesus in his humility, especially when I face opposition for speaking the truth.

JESUS CARRIES THE CROSS

Dear Mother Mary, help me accept the crosses God chooses for me, remembering Jesus will never leave me nor forsake me.

JESUS DIES ON THE CROSS

Dear Mother Mary, please grant to all humanity the grace of repentance, conversion, and final salvation.

The Glorious Mysteries
(Sunday, Wednesday)

THE RESURRECTION

Dear Mother Mary, please intercede with me for the grace of a strong and vibrant faith in the God who has won my redemption!

THE ASCENSION

Dear Mother Mary, help us to know His abiding presence and peace as we seek to be Christ to others.

THE DESCENT OF THE HOLY SPIRIT

Dear Mother Mary, please pray for the Spirit to anoint me with the fire of God's love and truth to bring His Kingdom to all.

THE ASSUMPTION OF MARY

Dear Mother Mary, help me be faithful to God's Will that I may someday reign in heaven with you.

THE CORONATION OF MARY

Dear Mother Mary, wrap us in your mantle of love that we may always proclaim the greatness of the Lord and rejoice in His salvation. He loves us! Amen!

The Chaplet of The Divine Mercy

For private recitation on ordinary rosary beads Our Father..., Hail Mary..., the Apostles' Creed.

Then, on the Our Father beads you will pray the following words:
Eternal Father, I offer You the Body and Blood, Soul and Divinity of Your dearly beloved Son, Our Lord Jesus Christ, in atonement for our sins and those of the whole world.

On the Hail Mary beads you will pray the following words:
For the sake of His sorrowful Passion, have mercy on us and on the whole world.

In conclusion three times you will pray these words:
Holy God, Holy Mighty One, Holy Immortal
One, have mercy on us and on the whole
world.

"The Chaplet of The Divine Mercy" is excerpted
from *Divine Mercy in My Soul: The Diary of
Saint Faustina M. Kowalska,* copyright 1987,
printed with permission of the Marian
Fathers of the Immaculate Conception,
Stockbridge, MA 01263.

How to Bless Your Family

God loves to bless us! As His first act after
creating us, God blessed us, by imparting to
us a portion of His creating power.

We strongly encourage you to put up a holy
water font in your home and to regularly
bless yourselves, your children, and others,
with the Sign of the Cross. As parents you
have the unique privilege of blessing your
children, calling down upon them the favor
and protection of God.

The traditional way to impart this blessing is
to have your child kneel. Lay your hands on

your child's head, and then bless your child with the Sign of the Cross on the child's forehead while praying:

"May the Almighty God, Father, Son, and Holy Spirit, bless you, my child, for time and eternity, and may this blessing remain forever with you. Amen."

Building Traditions of Prayer

Here are some suggested steps for family prayer:

- **Set a special time.** Keep in mind that you want to create a habit of prayer, so pick a time that works for everyone, as much as possible.
- **Decide on a "sacred space."** This is very important. Set aside a small table or alcove at which you can pray as a family.
- **Set up a family altar.** Put up an image of Jesus or Mary, or both! Select some smaller images or icons, candles and the Bible, and perhaps some rosaries.
- **Talk about prayer with your family.** Share that God is a Person who wants to hear from us and speak to us.

- **Start simple.** Be patient. For instance, you might begin with a few traditional prayers and build to actually praying a decade or more of the Rosary.
- **Give every person a chance to pray out loud.** God likes to hear from everyone, especially the little ones. However, do not force anyone to pray out loud.
- **Never use prayer as a time to scold or lecture any family member.** Prayer is a loving and intimate communion with God, not a soapbox. If you need to correct someone, stop the prayer, discipline your child, and return to prayer.
- **Don't give up! Try to pray every day.** However, if you miss a day, just pick it up again the next day. One fall doesn't make a failure!
- **Something is better than nothing.** Even if sometimes the prayer time is shorter or not everyone can make it, just by gathering together you will be gladdening the heart of God and affirming your habit of prayer.
- **Use sacramentals.** Bless each member of the family with holy water and light a blessed candle nightly. Use an Advent wreath in the four weeks before Christmas.

Bring home blessed palms and weave them into crosses during Holy Week. These are only a few of the many sacred objects and actions which the Church provides for us. Sacramentals impart grace according to the prayer of the Church and our own faith, and are a powerful reminder of God's abundant favor.

Living the Liturgical Seasons

Our worship as Catholic Christians follows an annual cycle of the mysteries in the lives of Jesus and Mary, along with feasts of the angels and the saints, known as the Liturgical Year. We encourage you to change the colors of your family altar coverings and add candles or sacramentals of the season.

ADVENT

In Advent we remember Jesus' first coming and prepare for His Second Coming. Advent's color is violet. Set up an Advent Wreath with four candles representing the four weeks of Advent. Three of the candles are purple, reminding us to pray and offer up little sacrifices to prepare the way for Jesus.

The third candle is rose, reminding us to be joyful since the birth of Jesus is drawing near. Put up an Advent Calendar—with 24 numbered flaps concealing a bible scene and Scriptural prophecy or verse—on the prayer table or wall. Let each family member take a turn opening a new door and reading the verse as Christmas draws near.

CHRISTMAS

Christmas is the most wonderful time of the year! Replace the Advent candles with white ones and place a Christ Candle in the middle. Light the wreath daily during the Christmas season, which lasts until the Baptism of the Lord. Pray a blessing over your Christmas tree and set up a Nativity scene or crèche underneath it.

LENT

Lent begins with Ash Wednesday. During these 40 days, we are called to open our hearts more deeply to God's fervent love through the ancient practices of prayer, fasting, and almsgiving. This would be a great time to receive the Sacrament of Reconciliation as a family in preparation for the celebration of Christ's Passion, Death, and Resurrection.

Jesus calls us to care for the poor with material blessings given from our heart. A great family project would be to put money saved by fasting during Lent into a "bank" and then give it to the poor.

EASTER!

Easter is the premier feast of our faith. He is risen, as He said! Alleluia! Here are some ways to celebrate the "definitive victory" of Christ Jesus over every difficulty, sin, illness, and challenge we face:

• Light a Christ candle for the Easter season.
• Pray the Regina Coeli instead of the Angelus.

PENTECOST

On Pentecost, God sent forth His Spirit upon Mary and the apostles. Pentecost ends the Easter season and ushers us into the rest of the year with the dynamite power of the Holy Spirit!

ORDINARY TIME

The color for this season is green. It is all about an opportunity for growth and flourishing. Putting plants up in the house and spending time in nature are great ways to experience the way God's creation grows from a small seed into a beautiful plant. This is a good time to focus on establishing a routine of prayer.

Sunday: For God and Family

Therefore, you must keep the sabbath as something sacred. ... Six days there are for doing work, but the seventh day is the sabbath of complete rest, sacred to the LORD.
–Exodus 31:14-15

We read in Scripture that God invites us to keep the Sabbath as a day to rest and honor God. We who are redeemed by Jesus celebrate the Sabbath on Sunday, the day He rose triumphantly from the dead. In his Apostolic Letter, *Dies Domini*, Pope John Paul II invited us to see each Sunday as a celebration of Christ's Resurrection, and ourselves as the two disciples at Emmaus, who felt their hearts "burning within them" as they walked and talked with the risen Lord Jesus.

God wants to give us a gift—the gift of His Sabbath presence. We need to prepare for this gift. We need to better understand this gift. Time with Him is our greatest treasure!

God wants us to enjoy even in this world the joy of His presence and the rest from our labors. Hence we need to do our best to finish our home and school work and prepare our home so we can ideally enjoy a special meal Saturday evening and usher in the blessing and restoration of the Lord's Day.

A great way to prepare for Sunday is to read in advance the Scripture readings proclaimed at Mass and to talk about them as a family. Sunday is a time to come as children to our Father and to receive again His healing, merciful, life-giving, and truly satisfying presence.

Jesus is our Divine Bridegroom, and we are called to be His true and loyal spouse, looking only to Him who is the fulfillment of all desire.

Finally, Sunday is meant to be a day for others—to be open for ways to sacrificially give of ourselves to the needy among us.

Reach out to your extended family or those in need, especially the sick, the elderly, children, and immigrants.

Prayer of a Family in Crisis

Loving Father, You know the crisis which has descended upon and into our family. Our minds are spinning, our souls are in turmoil, we are besieged by challenges we never suspected to visit us, and our very future seems cloudy and frightening. From the vortex of this distress we beg light to see more clearly, strength to respond as we should, and trust that You will see us through this.

May we never give up on You or on one another. Help us to love, not judge; encourage, not blame; embrace, not reject. According to Your will, O Father, restore us to peace, perhaps in different circumstances, but peace nonetheless. In Jesus' name. Amen.

Spiritual Armor Prayer
Adapted from Ephesians 6:10-18

Heavenly Father, we ask You today for Your truth as a belt tight around our waist. We put on the zeal to announce Your good news of peace as shoes for our feet.

We put on Your righteousness, O Christ, as our breastplate, and the hope of salvation as a helmet for our head.

Father, we take up faith as a shield which is able to put out all the fiery darts of the enemy, and the sword of the Spirit, which is Your Word, O Lord. Father, may the love with which You have loved Jesus be in us, and may Jesus be in us. We ask You for the grace of a servant heart. Amen.

Dear God, thank You for caring so much for us that You grant us all we need to stay strong in You! You are great, and greatly to be praised!

Prayer for a Happy Death

O Glorious Saint Joseph, Tradition tells us you gave your last breath in the loving embrace of Jesus and Mary. We rightly see that as "death as good as it gets." I choose you for my special patron in life and most of all at the hour of my death. Preserve and increase in me the spirit of prayer and fervor in the service of God. Remove far from me every kind of sin.

Obtain for me that my death may not come upon me unawares, but that I may have time to confess my sins sacramentally and to lament them with perfect understanding and sincere and perfect contrition, in order that I may breathe forth my soul into the hands of Jesus and Mary. Amen.